Montego F. R. Craddock

I0487610

EYES

on the

PRIZE

A Step-By-Step Approach To Winning The Job

Outskirts Press, Inc.
Denver, Colorado

Eyes on the Prize
A Step-By-Step Approach To Winning The Job

Outskirts Press, Inc.
http://www.outskirtspress.com

ISBN: 978-1-4327-2011-7

Library of Congress Control Number: 2008921558

Outskirts Press and the "OP" logo are trademarks belonging to Outskirts Press, Inc.

PRINTED IN THE UNITED STATES OF AMERICA

If you would like to share your success with other job seekers and or would like to have an Eyes on the Prize seminar workshop at your school, or organization please e-mail your request at eyesontheprize07@yahoo.com

Table of Contents

Acknowledgment   i

Preface   iii

Researching The Position   1

Analyzing Your Strengths & Weaknesses   5

Job Resources   9

Researching Companies   15

Men's Dress Attire   21

Women's Dress Attire   25

High School Dress Attire   29

Job Application   33

Cover Letter   39

Resumes   49

Electronic Resume   73

Interviewing Techniques   83

Thank You Letter   101

Salary Negotiation   105

Letter of Acceptance   109

Job Rejection Follow-Up Letter   111

Job Refusal Letter   113

Summary   115

Acknowledgment

To my lovely wife and best friend, **Alonna L. Craddock** who has given me something I have always wanted a beautiful family. I thank you for bringing so much joy to my life and thank you for encouraging me to complete this book and assisting in proofreading it.

This book is also dedicated to **Amonte**, **Aiyannah**, **Montego Jr.**, **Dante**, **Devon**, **Miracal**, **Mahdika**, **Quanitta** and **Hazzauna**. I am truly blessed to have you all as my family. I love you all.

To my mother, **Vurdis Craddock**, thank you for being the **best mother in the world.**

To my sisters and brothers thank you for always being supportive.

Preface

If you are unemployed, changing jobs, or need to improve your job search skills for today's job market and want to learn how to win the job, then this book is for you.

Winning the job does not mean there's a job guarantee, but it does mean preparing yourself to succeed in obtaining a job. Succeeding in the job market means focusing on the tools that are needed to increase the odds, overcome obstacles, surpass competition, and ultimately land the job.

"The fight is won or lost far away from witnesses behind the lines, in the gym, and out there on the road, long before I dance under those lights." - Muhammad Ali.

A fighter prepares for a fight through rigorous training. He conditions his body to endure punishment and builds the stamina to go the distance. He then puts together a plan to win the fight.

You, the applicant, must go through preparation and then develop a **plan** to win the job.

You begin by having a positive **attitude**, **confidence**, and **claiming** the position long before the interview.

Never lose your confidence, even if you are not getting responses to your inquiries or interviewers select someone else for positions. Don't take it personally.

Always remember two things:

1. If you're not selected, it's their loss.
2. There are interviewers searching for your skills and personality.

Be patient, assertive, persistent, consistent, and keep your "Eyes on the Prize."

Researching
The Position

The **first step** in preparing to win the job is to make sure you have the qualifications necessary to perform the job. It is important to research the position you are seeking. You need to know the following:

1. Job Specifications
2. Job Description
3. Average Salary
4. Employment Outlook

Job Specifications are the education, work experience, training, and licenses required to perform the job.

The Job Description (or Job tasks) is usually a narrative description of the responsibilities for a position.

Average Salary As an applicant, it is crucial that you know what the average salary is for a prospective position. The average salary serves as a basis for salary negotiation: you will use it as a starting range. **Example:** $18,000 to $20,000 or $10.00 to $15.00 an hour

Employment Outlook is the prospect for growth and long-term stability in a field. What does the future hold for this position?

Having this information at hand will help you to scrutinize your strengths and weaknesses, better prepare for the job interview, and make a rational career decision. For those of you who are not sure which career area interests you, there is a website that can assist you. Go to **Project Career** at www.projectcareer.com.

ALSO, HERE ARE HELPFUL REFERENCES AVAILABLE AT MOST PUBLIC LIBRARIES AND ON THE INTERNET TO HELP YOU IN YOUR PREPARATION:

1. **The American Almanac of Jobs & Salaries**, by John W. Wright and Edward J. Dwyer.

2. **Occupational Outlook Handbook**, compiled by the United States Department of Labor. at www.bls.gov/oco/

3. **Encyclopedia of Careers and Vocational Guidance** by William E. Hopke

4. **U.S. Department of Labor Bureau of Statistics website** at www.bls.gov/

5. **Highest Paying Jobs in the U.S.A.** www.whenpenguisattack.com/2006/11/24/highest-paying-jobs-in-the-us/

6. **Plunkett Research, Ltd.Website** www.plunkettresearch.com/Industries/MajorEmployers/tab id/78/Default.aspx

7. **Statistical Abstract of the United States**

8. **American Salaries & Wages Survey**

9. **Employment and Earnings** gives a monthly update of average hours and earnings for industries.

10. **Business Periodicals Index.**

11. **World Almanac and Book of Facts.**

12. **Information Please Almanac.**

13. **Universal Almanac.**

14. **O*NET Dictionary of Occupational Titles, Third Edition.**

15. **PayScale** provides accurate, real-time salary reports based on your job title, location, education, skills and experience. www.payscale.com/

Make sure to use the latest editions of these references.

"The will to win is not nearly as important as the will to prepare to win."
- Bobby Knight

Analyzing Your Strengths & Weaknesses

Those who fail to prepare for a job planned to fail on the interview.

The **second step** in preparing to win the job is to analyze your strengths and then your weaknesses.

Why? Because you are searching for that skill or talent that will give you a competitive edge and you'll have the chance to improve any weaknesses that can affect your presentation during the interview or performance on the job.

EXERCISE: Begin by brainstorming your skills and talents. List them below.

1._____

2._____

3._____

4._____

5._____

6._____

7._____

8._____

9._____

10._____

11._____

12._____

13._____

Review the list and select those skills that meet the job specifications. In addition, select four or five special skills that are not requirements, but that are your assets. You will use the information from your **research** about the position on **Pages 1, 2 and 3** to determine job specifications. Write your selections on the lines below.

Example: A receptionist needs good interpersonal and communication skills. If he is bilingual as well, this is an asset that will give him a competitive edge over other applicants who are not.

YOUR SKILLS THAT MATCH THE JOB SPECIFICATIONS

1._____

2._____

3._____

4._____

5._____

6._____

7._____

YOUR SPECIAL SKILLS

1._____

2._____

3._____

4._____

You will use these skills in your cover letter, resume, phone inquiries, and interview presentations, discussed in later chapters.

Next make a list of your weaknesses and\or skills that need improvement that can affect your work performance or presentation for the interview. **Be honest** and **specific**.

1._____

2._____

3._____

4._____

5._____

6._____

7._____

8._____

9._____

10._____

It is crucial that you work on improving these weaknesses before you go to an interview. If that means enrolling in seminars, classes, or workshops, then do so. You must be willing to invest in yourself to win the job.

8

Job Resources

The **third step** in preparing to win the
job is being **resourceful.** Resourcefulness means knowing where
to search for job opportunities. It's just like going fishing: if you
use the right bait, opportunity will come knocking. If you use the
wrong bait or fail to prepare, Murphy's Law will come knocking.
The more resources you are aware of, the greater chances of getting more interviews. The more interviews you can schedule, the
greater your chances of winning the job.

Remember, you are the bait and if you prepare correctly many fish
will bite.

It is important to use all of the following resources to gain optimal
results:

1. Major Newspapers, local newspapers, community newspapers, monthly government publications, trade magazines
   and journals. **When you are reviewing classified headings look under all possible related headings for a particular job. (Example:** Jobs for secretarial positions might
   be found under office work, receptionist, customer service,
   word processing, office clerk, data entry, and administrative assistant.) **Note:** Many newspapers and magazines are
   now on line.

2. **Networking** — is the best way of finding the hidden job
   markets (jobs that are not advertised). You can locate these
   jobs by networking with family members, friends, relatives,

pastors, barbers, beauticians, school counselors, and placement offices.

3. **The public library** — is another resource to use to collect information on companies in your state for cold calling (random phone inquiry) or mail inquiry. You will find many reference books for securing information on possible prospects. Speak with your reference desk librarian.

4. **The telephone directory** — is an excellent source for finding company names, numbers, and addresses for making job inquiries.

5. **Cable television and/or radio stations** — advertise job opportunities. Contact your local radio and cable companies.

6. **Chamber of Commerce** — You can ask about their member listing to get contact names for possible employment opportunities.

7. **City Hall, Hall of Records, county court buildings, and federal buildings** are sources to use for job inquiries.

8. **Pounding the payment** — is going door to door making job inquiries.

9. **Universities, state and community colleges** have job fairs. Contact their placement departments to find out when the next one will be held.

10. **Major job fairs** –are announced in your local and major newspapers.

11. **Private government, and temporary employment agencies,** — Private agencies sometimes charge a fee govern-

ment agencies do not. I would recommend temporary agencies for people who need to gain work experience. Sometimes, temporary jobs lead to permanent positions.

INTERNET RESOURCES

EMPLOYMENT RELATED WEBSITES:
a. www.careerbuilder.com **(CareerBuilder)**
b. www.hotjobs.com **(Hot jobs)**
c. www.monster.com **(Job search)**
d. www.jobsearch.org **(America's job bank)**
e. www.job.com **(Register and post resume)**
f. www.careerboard.com **(Job search and recommendations)**
g. www.topusajobs.com **(Search jobs by state category)**
h. www.summerjobs.com **(Seasonal employment)**
i. www.employmentguide.com **(Search jobs)**
j. www.jobbankusa.com **(Post resumes and search for jobs)**

COLLEGE WEBSITES:
a. www.collegerecruiter.com **(College career connector)**
b. www.collegjobboard.com **(Designed to help students and alumni find internships and temporary, part-time, and full-time jobs)**
c. www.aftercolleg.com **(Find jobs and internship)**

EXECUTIVE WEBSITES:
a. wwww.mbaexchange.com **(The MBA Exchange)**
b. www.6figurejobs.com **(Executive resources)**
c. www.mbajungel.com **(Career tools)**
d. www.execunet.com **(Exclusive network for executive jobs)**

SPECIALITY JOB TYPES:
  a. www.computerjobs.com **(Website focused solely on the IT industry)**
  b. www.healthcareresources.com **(Healthcare resources)**
  c. www.nursetown.com**(Jobs for the health care profession)**
  d. www.lawjobs.com **(Leading legal news and information)**
  e. www.careerbank.com **(Leading online career center for the accounting, finance, mortgage, insurance and banking community)**
  f. www.salesjobs.com **(Jobs in sales)**
  g. www.airlinecareer.com **(Airline jobs)**
  h. www.tvjobs.com **(Jobs in broadcasting)**

INTERNATIONAL WEBSITES:
  a. www.jobpilot.com **(international job pilot)**
  b. www.totaljobs.com **(Part of Total jobs Group Ltd, the UK's largest and fastest growing online recruitment company)**

1. **Write to Impact Publications:**
   9104 Manassas Drive, Suite N
   Manassas Park, VA 20111-5211
   Phone: 703-361-7300 - Fax: 703-335-9486
   The catalog contains almost every important career and job finding resource available today.
2. Some references above came from "**America's Top Internet Job Sites**" 2nd edition by Ron and Caryl Krannich, **PhDs** pages 23 to 25, a book I highly recommend for your reference library.

Remember, use all resources, prepare properly, and the right fish will come along. Fail to prepare and Murphy will come knocking.

Researching Companies

The **fourth step** in preparing to win the job is to research the company and the industry in which you are seeking employment. If the company is on the Fortune 500 list, it is mandatory to do research. If the company is a small one and you can't locate information, learn about its industry.

Why is it important to research a company before the interview?

1. One way to leave a lasting impression on an interviewer is to ask questions based on your research. That shows you're interested and that you are thorough.

2. Research will inform you about the company's philosophy, policies and procedures, dress codes if there are any, financial condition of the company, its ranking in the competitive market, plans for future growth, organizational structure and internal weakness or strengths.

What do you need to learn about the company?

1. **Brief history (What is the company primary purpose?)**
2. **Key executives**
3. **Location of corporate head quarters, and branches**
4. **Products and services offered. (Who are the company customers?)**

5. **Subsidiaries (Company's owned by the parent company)**

6. **Financial statements (Showing income statement, & balance sheet)**

7. **Competitive ranking in the industry**

8. **Organizational chart**

9. **Company's future plans**

10. **About the industry**

Yes, work is involved, and I can tell you many stories of my students who have taken the time to gather this information. These students were able to win the job even with no experience because of the questions they asked and because they made a positive impression.

Here are lists of references for locating information about companies:

Companies Publicly or Privately Owned/Closely Held:

Directory of companies required to file annual report with the Security Exchange Commission (S.E.C.).

Eyes on the Prize

Parent Company or Subsidiaries:

1. Directory of Corporate Affiliations
2. International Directory of Corporate Affiliations
3. American's Corporate Families

Types of Business, Executive Officers, Number of Employees, Annual Sales:

1. Standard & Poor's Register of Corporations
2. Dunn & Bradstreet's Million Dollar Directory
3. Ward's Business Directory of Largest U.S. Companies
4. Career Guide: Dunn's Employment Opportunities Directory
5. Standard Directory of Advertisers

Company's Background and Financial Data:

1. Standard & Poor's Corporate Records
2. Moody's Manual
3. Walker's Manual of Western Corporations

Company News Worthy:

1. Predicasts F & S Index
2. Business Periodicals Index

Company Listed in a Specialized Directory:

1. Thomas Register of American Manufacturers
2. Best's Insurance Reports
3. Standard Directory of Advertising Agencies
4. U.S.A. Oil Industry Directory
5. Who's Who in Electronics
6. Fairchild's Financial Manual of Retail Stores
7. World Aviation Directory

8. Medical & Health Care Market Place Guide

Company's Rank in the Industry:

1. Annual Issues of Fortune, Forbes, Inc., and Business Week
2. Dunn's Business Rankings

Note: Contact the reference librarian at your community or community college library to check on the availability and use of their references. Many libraries can direct you to computer services and databases on company profiles (for example, Thomas Gale Info Trac)—they save a tremendous amount of time. In addition, you can go to

- ✓ **Insider Partner (for company profiles) at www.insiderpartner.com/default.asp**
- ✓ **MANTA essential business information for free at www.manta.com/**
- ✓ **Free company profiles at www.finance.yahoo.com/q/pr?s=free**
- ✓ **Global corporate information on the leading companies in over 55 countries at**
  www.corporateinformation.com/
  www.forbes.com/lists,
  www.business.com,
  www.bizweb.com,
  www.fortune.com,
  www.thomasreginal.com
  www.thecorporatelibrary.com and
  www.moodys.com

You also can find information in the Business Almanac.

Some things get done badly because they are genuinely hard to do well, and some get done badly because nobody tried hard enough to do them well.

-By Bits & Pieces

Men's Dress Attire

The **fifth step** in preparing to win the job for both males and females is to wear appropriate dress attire to the interview. First impressions are important because you don't get a second chance. Whatever opinions you have about what you should wear on an interview, please disregard them and follow the suggestions listed below. The suggestions below are based on **facts**, and **they work**. This is no time for **experimenting**. You only get **one** chance. Make it your **best**.

It doesn't matter what type of job you want, you must always look **professional** and **conservative** for the interview. If you are pounding the pavement to complete applications, look professional and act as if you are in an interview. The screening process begins the moment you walk through the door to complete an application, and you are judged first by your appearance.

Someone said, "It's better to be prepared for an opportunity and not have one, than to have an opportunity and not be prepared."

Here are suggestions about what you should wear on the interview. Following this advice, will increase the number of points you receive at the interview for overall appearance.

1. The day before the interview, go to the barber to get a haircut and mustache or beard trim so that you have a fresh look. Shave either the night before or that morning.

2. Don't wear earrings or excessive jewelry, regardless of style.

3. Don't wear excessive cologne that arrives before you do.

4. Make sure your fingernails are clean and manicured.

5. Make sure your teeth are clean. Use mouthwash as opposed to chewing gum.

6. The three styles of suits are European, American, and British. Any will do. You can wear a single or doubled-breasted or three piece suit. If you don't have one of these, invest in one. A three piece suit is considered most conservative. The two preferred colors are navy blue and gray. They represent the corporate (conservative) look and are the working colors; however, you can wear other dark colors, except for black. Although black is a beautiful color, people associate it with funerals or formal occasions. If you decide to wear black anyway, breakup the colors. Perhaps you can wear black pants with different colored tweed, checkered, or plaid blazer. Pinstripes are OK. Or you can wear a blazer and slacks.

7. Wear a solid white dress shirt, with or without French cuffs. White symbolizes sincerity.

8. Wear a printed or solid color silk tie with matching handkerchief or a white handkerchief to match your white shirt.

9. Wear black socks to match your black shoes. The shoes should be wing tips and they may have tassels or ruffles. These shoes styles are considered conservative.

10. Carry an attaché case or briefcase. The preferred colors are brown or black.

11. During the wintertime, wear a dress coat or heavy trench coat.

Women's Dress Attire

Women's clothing is more fashionable than men's, so you have more options. But the key is still a conservative appearance and hair style. The suggestions below are based on facts and they're proven effective.

1. Before the interview go to your beautician and get your hair done, nails manicured and filed to a normal length. Remember to have a conservative hair style: you can ask beautician for ideas for styles that will become you.

2. Don't wear excessive makeup. You are not going to a circus.

3. Don't wear red, hot pink, or any other brightly colored lipstick. Your lipstick should be a natural or dark color. Again, consult your cosmetologist. Your fingernails should match your lipstick to show color coordination. If you don't wear makeup, that's fine: perhaps you can use lip gloss and wear a transparent finger nail polish. Don't go heavy on the lip gloss; you don't want to look greasy.

4. Don't wear dangling earrings, or earrings that display your name or the name of your boyfriend, a religious group or an organization. Wear post earrings or small hoops; these are more conservative. No excessive jewelry.

5. Don't wear perfumes or oils that arrive before you do.

6. The two preferred colors for your clothing are **navy blue** and **gray** but other dark colors like **olive green**, **burgundy**, and **dark tan** are acceptable. Pinstripes or plaid are O.K.

7. It is preferable to wear a skirt suit, or blazer and skirt because these present a more professional appearance compared with dresses or a blouse and skirt. Don't wear miniskirts. Your skirt length should be slightly above the knee cap, or slightly below the knee cap. Don't wear long skirts. If you have a split in your skirt, make sure it's no more than four inches.

8. Wear a white dress blouse because it represents sincerity and make sure you wear a black or beige brassiere underneath. Don't wear ruffles, shiny materials, or lace; you are not going to a party or club.

9. Wear skin-tone stockings or those that blend with your skin. Don't wear colored stockings, lace, or net hosiery as these are not conservative attire.

10. Wear pumps or leather shoes with heels no higher than two or three inches (No flats). Your shoes may match your skirt suit, blazer and skirt or dress and blazer.

11. Carry an attaché case or portfolio rather than your purse; you will look more professional. You can put your personal belongings in your attaché or portfolio case. The two preferred colors are black or brown. Don't carry large bags or a purse with your attaché case. You are not a bag lady.

12. During winter months wear a dress coat or heavy trench coat.

Aim high! It is no harder to shoot the feathers off an eagle than to shoot the fur off a skunk.

- Troy Moore

High School Dress Attire Pointers For The Interview

If you are a high school student, it is important to remember even though you are applying for an entry-level job, your appearance, etiquette skills, and resume are just as important as if you were applying for an executive-level position. Why? Because these things reflect your character and inform the interviewer what you're like.

They will also set you apart from all other applicants. Let's look at an example: Suppose you are applying for the cashier clerk position at McDonald's Restaurant. When you arrive for the interview, you notice that no other high school student is appropriately dressed—they are all wearing jeans and everyday casual clothes. You are dressed to impress, in a white shirt, tie, dress slacks or white blouse and skirt with dress shoes. Your resume is inside the portfolio case you're carrying, and you present yourself in a professional manner. You will stand out from the others and probably will be considered first for the position, because of the positive impression you've made.

Let's face it: most students do not understand that when you go to an interview, you should always be at your best (and when you get the job, give it your best!)

APPROPRIATE BUSINESS ATTIRE FOR TEENAGE GIRLS:

Montego F. R. Craddock

Shirts: knit shirts with collars, turtlenecks, mock neck, or jewel neck and of a dressy fabric, i.e. silk, cashmere, and wool blends. **Blouses**, twin sets, jackets or cardigan sweaters also are acceptable. **NO denim jackets.**

Bottoms: Classic skirts, dress slacks (plain or pleated front) of wool blends, cotton, or micro fiber. Leather or suede skirts should be professional-style. **NO denim skirts.**

Dresses: Casual classic dresses, sheath style with blazers, 2-piece or 3-piece suit, cardigans or business style are acceptable.

Shoes: Loafers, heels, dress boots, and oxfords are acceptable.

Accessories: Hosiery appropriate to the outfit is required"

Inappropriate items include: revealing necklines, sheer fabrics, midriffs (any blouse that exposes your belly is unacceptable), plain cotton T-shirts, flannel, fleece, sweatshirts or sweatpants, tank tops or halters. **Unacceptable bottoms** are Capri pants, shorts or overalls. **Unacceptable dresses** are mini or halter dresses and sun dresses. **Unacceptable shoes** are athletic shoes of any type, thong/flip-flop style sandals, and clogs.

(Source for this page: Top Teens of America Dress Attire, www.tlod.org/Syn-Lod-Attire-Teens-2007.html)

APPROPRIATE BUSINESS ATTIRE FOR TEENAGE BOYS:

Please view and read text box at the bottom of page 31.

HIGH SCHOOL DRESS ATTIRE
FOR THE INTERVIEW
(Young Men)

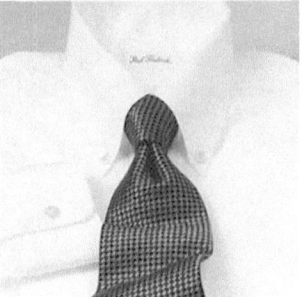

Professional business attire consists of **dress shirts and ties** for boys, with suits or coordinated sport coats and slacks. (It is preferred that boys wear coats at all times).

Some Images retrieved from Paul Fredrick at www.paulfredrick.com//Catalog/PFCategory.aspx?Category=basics and Text Tile Trading at www.suitbusiness.com/TTA%20Mens%20Suits.html

HIGH SCHOOL DRESS ATTIRE
FOR THE INTERVIEW
(Young Women)

The professional business attire for girls consists of dresses, skirt/blouse coordinates, business suits, pantsuits, or dress slacks and blouses, along with panty hose at all times.

Job Application

The **sixth step** in preparing to win the job is to **accurately** and **neatly** complete a job application. The application is another screening tool used by the interviewer to determine whether to grant you an interview. The way you complete the application is a reflection of yourself.

Here are rules to remember to ensure success:

1. Read carefully, follow instructions, and be honest.

2. Write the correct date.

3. **Never Ever** complete an application with a **pencil.** This is an **important document;** treat it as such. Use a **black pen**.

4. Complete the entire application, providing any and all necessary information. (Job dates, telephone numbers, addresses, supervisor's names, and at least three references) Make sure to include volunteer work if it relates to the job. Volunteer work is unpaid work experience. Volunteering also makes a positive statement about you.

5. To aid you in completing job applications in person or online create an index card, which will be your information tool card providing you with information you sometimes forget, or can't recall. You can also use your Palm Pilot.

Your index card contains the following:

> Social security number:
>
> Driver's license number:
>
> Three reference names: Job titles, addresses, & telephone numbers
>
> School and Job information:
>
> If you are using a functional resume, starting and ending salaries for previous jobs:

Most of the information will come from your resume. You will transfer the information from your index card or palm pilot to your job application, thus saving time, improving accuracy, and eliminating errors.

6. Don't volunteer information; just answer questions that apply to you, If they don't apply, write N/A (not applicable) on the line.

7. Another way interviewers screen applicants is to ask them about their salary requirements. Never write a salary in this blank instead write "open" (open for discussion), or "negotiable." At this point in the game, salary isn't important; what you need is an opportunity to show the interviewer what you can do for the company.

8. Don't scribble over an error or ask the receptionist for another application.

Eyes on the Prize

Example:

Correct your errors by drawing a neat line across the error and writing the correction above it.

9. Never ask the receptionist or secretary for the current date. If you don't know it, use another method to find it. Purchase a daily reminder calendar, or use your cell phone or palm pilot.

10. Make sure you sign the application and enter the current date.

11. Review your application to ensure accuracy before submitting.

On the next two pages is a sample application. Complete the application for practice, and use it as a guide to write your information index card.

Some people never hear opportunity knock, because they're too busy knocking opportunity.
    - Hal Chadwick

SAMPLE JOB APPLICATION

Sample Job Application

Fill out this sample application using your personal information. Include all applicable information and addresses.

PLEASE NOTE: Complete all parts of the application. If your application is incomplete, or does not clearly show the experience and/or training required, your application may not be accepted. If you have no information to enter in a section, please write N/A.

Name and Address	
Name (First, MI, Last)	Social Security Number
Mailing Address	
City, State, and Zip Code	
Home Phone	Message Phone
E-mail Address	May we use e-mail to contact you? Yes ☐ No☐

Additional Information
Have you been an employee of this organization in the past?   Yes ☐   No ☐
I certify that I am in compliance with the provisions of the Selective Service Act (Draft Registration). ** Yes ☐   No☐
I certify that I am a U.S. citizen, permanent resident, or a foreign national with authorization to work in the United States. ** Yes ☐   No☐
Have you ever been convicted of, or entered a plea of guilty, no contest, or had a withheld judgment to a felony? ** Yes ☐ No☐   If Yes, please explain:
** These questions must be answered in order to be considered for employment

Education (Schools attended or special training received)			
School	From	To	Did you graduate?
Location		Type of degree or diploma	
School	From	To	Did you graduate?
Location		Type of degree or diploma	

SAMPLE JOB APPLICATION

Work History				
JobTitle	From	To	Hrs/Week	Employer
Address	Phone	Supervisor		May we contact this employer? Yes ☐　　　No☐
Reason for leaving?				

Job Title	From	To	Hrs/Week	Employer
Address	Phone	Supervisor		May we contact this employer? Yes ☐　　　No☐
Reason for leaving?				

Job Title	From	To	Hrs/Week	Employer
Address	Phone	Supervisor		May we contact this employer? Yes ☐　　　No☐
Reason for leaving?				

How did you find out about this position?				
Current Employee ☐	Career Fair ☐	State website ☐	Company Newsletter ☐	Job Service ☐
Monster.com ☐	Newspaper Ad ☐	Other Internet Source ☐	Prof. Organization website ☐	Radio/TV Ad ☐
	Recruiter ☐	University/College ☐	None of the above ☐	

Job Type/Shift				
Full Time ☐	Part Time ☐	Permanent ☐	Temporary ☐	6 Month ☐
9 Month ☐	Seasonal ☐	Limited Service ☐	Shift ☐	Night ☐

Signature	Date

I certify that all answers and statements on this application are true and complete to the best of my knowledge. I understand that should an investigation disclose untruthful or misleading answers, my application may be rejected, my name removed from consideration, or my employment with this company terminated.

Cover Letter

The **seventh step** in preparing to win the job is to write an effective cover letter. A cover letter is a sales letter. Its purpose is to get attention, stimulate interest, and motivate the reader to review your resume. If impressed with your resume, the interviewer will follow up with you for an interview. Do not **sabotage** your job-hunting efforts by mailing a resume without a cover letter, or worse, with a hastily written one. A well-written letter can offset the tone of the impersonal resume and place you on "human terms" with the prospective employer. A cover letter allows you to tailor your interest to a particular opening—this is virtually impossible and impractical to do with a resume alone. You will use a cover letter to inquire about a job, respond to a classified ad or electronic ad via the Internet, or inquire about a job based on word of mouth.

COVER LETTER PROCESS

The ingredients that make up a cover letter are **introduction, body,** and **closing**.

Introduction: If you are applying for a specific position, identify the job by title and state how you heard about it. If you are not applying for a specific job, explain that you are not seeking a particular position and are writing to inquire whether the organization has any openings.

Body: List your qualifications and special skills for the position in summary form. If you are still a student or recent graduate and have had little work experience in a related field, focus on your education and training. If you have been employed in a related field, emphasize your work background. Then refer the reader to the resume for other important details.

When you are writing the body of a cover letter, think about job specification requirements. Your research on **page 1** will assist you in this area, or if requirements are from an ad in the paper, write several main qualities that you have that match the job specification. Then include several special skills that are not requirements, but are assets from **page 7**. When the interviewer reads the body of your cover letter, he or she will know you not only meet job specifications, but have other related skills as well. That's an asset.

Closing: State where you can be reached and when you will be available for an interview.

RULES TO FOLLOW

1. **Job applicants make sure your cover letter is brief, grammatically correct, and to the point. Your page should have a one inch margin all around. Use a word processor to draft your cover letter, or have it processed professionally by a print shop or resume service.**
2. **Use quality paper of 100 percent cotton fiber, and make sure you use the same paper for your resume and matching envelope.**

3. **Make sure your documents are printed on a laser jet printer.**

Eyes on the Prize

See the sample cover letters on the next few pages.

Then complete the Cover Letter Worksheet.

To build may have to be slow and laborious task of years. To destroy can be the thoughtless act of a single day.   By Winston Churchill

(Sample Cover Letter Responding to an Ad)

August 7, 2008

Mr. Bob Miller, Personnel Manager
Mechanical Systems Inc.
357 Park Drive
Richmond, NY 78965

Dear Mr. Miller:

I have enclosed a copy of my resume for your review and consideration for the bookkeeping position advertised in the "Star-Ledger" on September __, 2007.

I would like to point out the areas of skills and achievement in my background that are most relevant to the bookkeeping position.

– Over 10 years' bookkeeping experience for a variety of businesses

– Over 5 years' full-charge bookkeeping experience with computerized accounting systems

– Familiarity with PC-DOS operating systems and Peach Tree Accounting for Windows

– Exceptionally organized and resourceful with a wide variety of skills

I would appreciate a personal interview with you to discuss my application further. You can reach me at my home number (212) 345-4567 or office number during regular business hours,
(212) 567-6789.

Sincerely,

John Doe

(Sample Cover Letter
of Telephone Follow-up)

August 7, 2008

Mrs. Mary Prune, Personnel Manager
Law Firm of America
2345 Aims Street
Newark, NJ 07102

Dear Ms. Prune:

Thank you for speaking with me today about paralegal opportunities in your firm. Should a vacancy arise, I would appreciate being considered. I would bring to your firm the following qualifications:

> **Law:** Completed 40 semester hours of criminal justice course work with special emphasis on criminal law. Served as an intern with a law firm specializing in criminal law.

> **Research:** Conducted research on several high profile criminal cases as both a student and paralegal intern.

> **Communication:** Prepared research papers, legal summaries, memos, and briefed attorneys on criminal cases relevant to assignments.

Please let me know if you need any additional information. I will periodically check with you concerning impending vacancies. You can reach me at my home address, or (201) 786-7896.

Sincerely,

John Doe

Montego F. R. Craddock

(Sample Cover Letter)

August 7, 2008

Personnel Manager
Box 000
340 Spring Road
Valley, KY 10245

Dear Sir or Madam:

Enclosed is my resume for your review. Please consider my qualifications for the clerical word processing position advertised in the *New York Times* September 15, 2007.

I have three years of experience as a secretary for J & B Associates and a certificate in word processing from Technical Institute. I received extensive training in office procedures, and communications and I am proficient in Microsoft Office software programs.

I look forward to hearing from you soon. I can be reached at (201) 564-9000 or my office, (201) 765-0071, during regular business hours.

Sincerely,

Mary Doe

Cover Letter Work Sheet

Your Name

Address

City & State Zip Code

Date_____

Name of Person_____

Title_____

Company Name_____

Address_____

City State Zip Code_____

Dear_____:

Introduction_____

_____

Body_____

_____

Montego F. R. Craddock

_____

_____

_____

Closing_____

_____

_____

Sincerely,

Cover Letter Worksheet

Your Name_____

Address_____

City & State Zip Code_____

DATE_____

Name of Person_____

Title_____

Company Name_____

Address_____

City State Zip Code_____

Dear_____:

Introduction_____

_____

Related Job Skill _____

_____

Montego F. R. Craddock

Related Job Skill _____

_____

Related Job Skill _____

_____

Closing_____

_____

Sincerely,

Resumes

The **eighth step** in preparing to win the job is to create an **effective** resume. The purpose of a resume is to get an interview; there is no other purpose. Take your resume seriously, especially if you want the interviewer to take you seriously. It's been said that the average resume reader has no more than 30 to 45 seconds to look at a resume and decide whether it warrants further attention. Therefore, it is to your advantage to show off the best of your abilities. Your resume is a self-marketing tool. It should be lean and to the point, but remember this is not the time to be modest.

Do not write a general resume to fit all jobs. That shortcut, in my opinion, doesn't work. Customize your resume to fit the job you are seeking. If you must create several resumes, then do so.

There are four formats for resumes: **Chronological, Functional, Combination and Electronic.**

Chronological Resume: The best-known and widely used. It calls for the subject's most recent information and experience to be listed first, and then moves backward. Data **"dates are highlighted"**, and the writer must explain any obvious gaps in his work history. Employers respond well to the chronological format because it allows them to easily review the applicant's career progress from one step to the next.

Functional Resume: Places important emphasis on the individual's overall skills and abilities. The work history is defined by specific examples and responsibilities. Dates are omitted; previous positions may or may not be included.

Combination Resume: Has gained wide appeal over the years. It not only stresses the applicant's transferable skills (talents that may be used at a variety of jobs), but pinpoints job titles, dates, and past employers. This style is good for the entry-level applicants because it offers both direction and depth of experience.

Electronic Resume: With the growing use of the Internet as a tool in the job search process, it is a good idea to have your resume ready for the online global job market.

Reasons to have an electronic resume include these:

1. You can send your resume to networking contacts or recruiting professionals by e-mail.

2. You can place your resume in many databases with the hope that employers or recruiters will read it and call you in for an interview.

For more information please read page 73 about electronic resumes.

RULES FOR CREATING AN EFFECTIVE RESUME

1. A resume should fit on one 8- 1/2 by 11inch page, unless you have extensive background in education and professional work experience. Example: If you have a BA, MBA, PhD and membership, & 20 or more years of experience, then two pages should be the maximum. Set your margins for 1 inch or 1/2 inch all around.

2. If you have several degrees it is not necessary to list your high school.

3. Invest in quality paper, 100 percent cotton fiber with matching envelopes.

4. Resume paper should be light-colored, like ivory, cream, off white, beige, tan, or white. For paper styles, choose from classic laid, certificate bond, linen, and granite.

5. Print your resume on a **laser printer** for the best results, or have it professionally processed by a resume service company. You can use desk jet ink, to give the resume a laser look.

6. If you have no work experience, emphasize your education and training. If you have very little education, emphasize your work experience. If they are equal, it doesn't matter which is listed first.

7. **Education:** A history of your education and training (high school, trade school, and/or college).

8. **Work Experience:** A chronological list of places worked, responsibilities, and accomplishments.

9. Some employment consultants feel an objective is not needed in your resume. Others feel it's necessary to includes one. The argument against having one is that it limits you to a specific position, whereas you may be qualified for more than one related position. On the other hand, an objective is like a topic sentence and your education, skills, and experience must support it. Whether to use an objective will continue to be debated. It's your choice. A clearly stated objective can be very effective.

10. Review sample resumes beginning on page 60 and make your own decision.

Montego F. R. Craddock

There is nothing so fatal to character as half-finished tasks.
- David Lloyd George

11. If you have gaps in your resume, use the number of months and years you spent at each job, rather than the dates you worked there. **Example**: Don't use "September 1994 to September 1995"; instead, use "1 year" or 2 years, 6 months, etc.). An alternative is the functional resume style.

12. In the education section, write the year you graduated. It is not necessary to write the dates to and from.

13. When listing your job responsibilities and accomplishments start each sentence with an action verb. When you use active or action verbs you demonstrate how you made things happen and that you didn't just watch things happen around you. Use adverbs to liven up your achievements.

Eyes on the Prize

Examples: **Created** and managed a successful business.
Established unique new programs, and internships.
Continually developed work flow patterns to increase productivity.
Successfully increased sales by 20 percent in a month.

Montego F. R. Craddock

Here are lists of **action verbs:**

Communication Skills
addressed
arbitrated
arranged
authored
collaborated
convinced
correspond
directed
drafted
edited
enlisted
formulated
influenced
lectured
mediated
moderated
negotiated
persuaded
publicized
recruited
spoke
translated

interpreted
investigated
organized
reviewed
summarized
surveyed
systematized

Technical Skills
assembled
build
calculated
computed
devised
engineered
fabricated
maintained
operated
overhauled
programmed
remodeled
repaired
upgraded

Research Skills
clarified
collected
critiqued
diagnosed
evaluated
examined
extracted
identified
inspected

Teaching Skills
adapted
advised
clarified
coached
communicated
coordinated
demystified
developed
referred

Eyes on the Prize

enabled
encouraged
evaluated
explained
facilitated
guided
informed
instructed
persuaded
stimulated
trained

Financial Skills
administered
allocated
analyzed
appraised
audited
balanced
budgeted
calculated
computed
developed
forested
managed
marketed
planned
projected
research

Artistic Skills
acted
conceptualized
created
designed
developed

directed
established
fashioned
founded
illustrated
instituted
integrated
introduced
invented
originated
performed
planned
revitalized
shaped

Assisting Skills
assessed
assisted
clarified
coached
counseled
demonstrated
diagnosed
educated
expedited
facilitated
guided
motivated
rehabilitated
represent

Office Skills
approved
arranged
classified

collected
compiled
dispatched

Management Skills
administered
analyzed
assigned
attained
chaired
consolidated
contracted
coordinated
delegated
directed
evaluated
executed
improved
increased
organized
oversaw

planned
prioritized
produced
recommend
reviewed
scheduled
strengthen

Accomplishement
expanded
improved
pioneered
reduced
resolved
restored
transformed

Source: The Damn Good Resume by Yana Parker, page 54.

For more in-depth information on resume writing, I highly recommend the following books and websites: These books helped me to expand upon my ideas for **Eyes on the Prize.**

- **The Damn Good Resume Guide** By Yana Parker, www.damngood.com/ready/exmpl/references-list.html
- **Resumes** by Susan Ireland www.susanireland.com/eresumework.htm
- **Distinctive Documents**, www.distinctiveweb.com /elecresume.htm

SAMPLES OF
CHRONOLOGICAL RESUME

Montego F. R. Craddock

Bobby Wright
45 West Lane Road
Ireland, New Jersey 90876
(231) 675-8976

EMPLOYMENT:

8/2001 to Present

Assistant Loan Officer
Federal Savings of New York, Manhattan, New York

* Approved consumer loan applications, assisted customers.
* Analyzed customers financial statements for sound loan decision.
* Prepared written and oral reports for bank management.

9/1990-6/2001

Student Loan Manager
Savings & Loan Bank, Newark, New Jersey

* Calculated student loan portfolio yields.
* Budgeted loan sales over a three year period.
* Designed and conducted student seminars.

6/1994-5/2000

Management Trainee
Accounting Associates, Maple wood, New Jersey

* As a manager trainee became familiar with various departments including bookkeeping, customer service, and collections.

EDUCATION:

May 2000

St. John's College, New York, New York
B.S. Accounting
Dean's List

June 1999

American Institute of Banking, New York, NewYork
Certification
Bank Management, Accounting, Business Math, and English

June 1994

St. Luke's High School, Newark, New Jersey
Diploma

REFERENCES AVAILABLE UPON REQUEST

Eyes on the Prize

NECHOLES KYTHREETIS

23 West 45th Street   **Telephone:**
Bayonne, New Jersey 07002   (201) 833-3218

OBJECTIVE: Position as Transportation/Cargo Specialist.

HIGHLIGHTS OF QUALIFICATIONS

- ♦ Seven years experience working for the federal government in transportation.
- ♦ General office skills, warehouse management and terminal operation skills.
- ♦ Award for excellent customer service and job performance.
- ♦ Reliable, adaptable, accurate & an effective team player.

PROFESSIONAL EXPERIENCE

MILITARY OCEAN TERMINAL, CARGO OPERATIONS DIVISION, Bayonne, NJ
2000-present Shipping Clerk
- Interfaced with commercial carrier industry, ocean carrier and trucking companies.
- Monitored stevedoring, terminal operating contracts and contractor performance.
- Conducted warehouse and pier wall-to-wall inventories inspection of all government cargo.
- Supervised vessel loading operations on a periodic basis.
- Staged and segregated dangerous/hazardous cargo by type and stowage classification.
- Utilized automated computer staging, and storage system (LOGMARS) during vessel loading.
- Prepared work orders for cargo contract carrier and correspondence/replies to supervisors.
- Transcribed data from commercial paper work to government documents using MILSTAMP.
Training: *Office Automation, Microsoft Windows/Word, cc Mail and Hazardous Training.*

E.J. KORVETTES WHSLE & DISTRIBUTION CENTER, Bayonne, New Jersey
1990-1999 Shipping/Receiving and Inventory Supervisor
- Shipping/Receiving import & export of domestic goods and manifest bills of lading.
- Made appointments for common carriers.
- Communicated to customers, vendors and through written correspondence.
- Controlled inventory, receiving and packing of goods.
- Delegated employees' daily responsibility.

EDUCATION

Mgm't/Finance (50 credit hrs) S. Wales College, United Kingdom, England   1996-2000
Diploma, American/Greek Academy, Lissosol, Greece   1995

REFERENCES FURNISHED UPON REQUEST

Montego F. R. Craddock

JACKALINE ELLY CLARK
411 Bergen Avenue Apt 1
Bayonne, NJ 07305
(201) 345-2088

SUMMARY OF QUALIFICATIONS

* 15 years experience working for the federal government in transportation.
* Proficient time management, Interpersonal and communication skills.
* Extremely open to change, innovative and a team player.
* General office skills & accurate math skills.

SPECIAL TRAINING: Certificate for, System Analysis for Transportation, Physical Distribution Management, Transportation Terminal Management and Export-Import Management.

SOFTWARE SKILLS: CONUS & Freight Movement System, Dbase III Plus, cc:Mail for Windows, Microsoft Word, Freelance Graphics, Excel, PowerPoint and Lotus 123.

PROFESSIONAL EXPERIENCE

MILITARY OCEAN TERMINAL, MTMC EASTER AREA, Bayonne, NJ 1980-present
1990-present   Freight Rate Specialist of Freight Traffic Management Division
♦ Use federal regulations, I.C.C., guides to perform routine rating, routing on general cargo, POV'S and household goods throughout CONUS.
♦ Provide comparative transportation costs to personal property branch.
♦ Maintain rating and routing of shipments within two days of receipt.
♦ Utilize full truckload capability, and stop-offs to save government funds.
♦ Prepare bills of lading for commercial, line haul carriers domestically & internationally.

1989-1990   Transportation Assistant/Lead Clerk   Freight Traffic Management Division
Accomplishment: *Preload over 200 POV'S and heavy lift equipment by rail daily for support of Desert Shield Desert Storm. Resulted in a promotion as Freight Rate Specialist.*
♦ Resolved discrepancies on TDR pertaining to astray and frustrating cargo.
♦ Edited exported materials for foreign military sales.
♦ Booked various shipments under the (MET) Mechanized Export Traffic Systems.

1987-1986   Procurement Clerk   Military SeaLift Command Contract Office
♦ Typed general correspondence, solicited awards & bids and revised/amended contracts.

1980-1986   Supply Clerk   Defense Storage Office
♦ Audited warehouse, debited contracts and processed/calculated receipts.

EDUCATION

Transportation/International Business, St. John's University-on site job training   93-95
Mathematics, Jersey City State College-Jersey City, New Jersey (25 credits)   81-83
Diploma, Snyder High School-Jersey City, New Jersey   1981

SAMPLES OF COMBINATIONAL RESUME

Montego F. R. Craddock

Khidijah Y. Adems
264 South 13ᵗʰ Street
Newark, New Jersey 07105   *Telephone*   (201) 224-1456

Objective: *Position as Office Clerk/Receptionist /General Office.*

OFFICE SKILLS
- Windows 98/XP/Vista, Microsoft Office 2003/2007 and Desktop Publishing.
- Communication/Interpersonal & Time Management Skills.
- Proofreading and Editing Skills.

EDUCATION

CLERICAL WORD PROCESSING TRAINING:
Record Management: Alphabetical, Numerical, Geographical, and Subject filing.
Financial Application: Recording and Calculating Petty Cash, Deposit Slips, Reconciling Bank Statements, Account Receivables and Payables.
Word Processing, Data Processing, and Information Processing.

Five weeks of hands on experience as a secretary/receptionist: Answering incoming phone calls, taking messages, transferring calls, assisting customers, storing and retrieving files, and copying/faxing documents, typing and processing various types of correspondence.

Certificate, Clerical Word Processing – CareerWorks, Inc. Newark, New Jersey   1/1995
Info., Science & Systems (24 credits) Morgan State University, Baltimore, MD   1992-1993
Diploma, College Prep/Business – Bernie L. Edmondson High School, E.O., NJ   1985-1992

EMPLOYMENT HISTORY

1993-Present   Cargo Handler Federal Express Corp., Newark, New Jersey
* Assorted packages according to URSA Code
* **April, 1994, Promoted to Checker/Sorter:** Operating handheld computer to scan packages
   for accuracy of City, State and Zip Code.

1992-1994   Sales/Cashier Clerk   S & A Stores, Orange, New Jersey
* Received customer service training operated cash register, stocked & arranged shelves.
* Handled money/credit transactions and made deposit of $3,000 - $5,000 into accounts.
*Checked inventory on a monthly basis, observed for shoplifting, worked as a liaison between staff & management.

1990-1991 Casual Mail Clerk   U.S. Postal Service, Newark, New Jersey
*Assorted and prepared mail for shipment.

References furnished upon request

Eyes on the Prize

Kamma V. Shawn

17 Seymore Avenue
Newark, New Jersey 08808
(264) 396-7988

Objective: Position as Clerical/Customer Service/General Office/Receptionist.

Clerical Word Processing Training

- **Type 45 WPM** with accuracy.
- **Software: Microsoft Office 2003/2007, Windows XP, and Desktop Publishing.**
- Interpersonal/communication skills, time management and word processing.
- Proofreading/editing documents, transcription and customer service.
- **Record Management:** Alphabetic, numerical, subject and geographical filing.
- **Financial Applications:** Recorded petty cash, deposit slips, reconciling bank statements, accounts receivables and payable.

Five weeks of hands on experience as a secretary/receptionist: Answering incoming phone calls, taking messages, transferring calls, faxing/copying documents storing/receiving files, typing and processing various types of correspondence.

Education

Certificate, Clerical Word Processing – CareerWorks, Inc., Newark, New Jersey   1/1995
Diploma, Business/College Prep – Malcolm X Shabazz, Newark, New Jersey   6/1983

Employment History

Material Handler, Ad-Aid, Newark, New Jersey   2/1993- 9/1993

Cashier, C Town, Newark, New Jersey   8/1991-12/1992
- Operated cash register and assisted customers.
- Always maintained accurate cash registered.
- Received customer service training: Emphasized providing quality customer service and defusing an irate customer.

Payroll Clerk, Affirmative Action Dept., City Hall, Newark, New Jersey   5/1992-12/1992
- 80% percent of responsibility included inputting data from payroll register into the computer.
- Answered incoming phone calls and took messages.
- Filed and copied documents.

SAMPLE OF
FUNCTIONAL RESUME

Montego F. R. Craddock

Metashya Wenbish

10 Roseville Avenue
Newark, New Jersey 07237

Telephone:
(201) 484-2111

Objective: Clerical/General Office/Receptionist

Clerical Word Processing Training

Computer Skills:
- Type 35 words per minute.
- MOS Certification (Microsoft Office 2003/2007), Windows XP and Desktop Publishing.

Office Procedures:
- Interpersonal communication skills, time management, and word processing.
- Record management: alphabetic, numeric, subject and geographical filing system.
- Financial application: Recording petty cash, deposit slips, reconciling bank statement, accounts receivable and payable.
- Customer Service Training.

Five weeks internship as a secretary/receptionist: Answering incoming phone calls, recording messages, and copying/faxing documents, assisting customers, retrieving/storing files, typing and processing correspondence.

Special Projects:
- Writing reports, proofreading and editing various types of business correspondence.
- Researching companies and transcribing dictation.
- Creating spreadsheets and graphics.

Education

Certificate, Clerical Word Processing – CareerWorks, Inc., Newark, New Jersey   1/2004
Diploma, Business/College Prep-West Side High School, Newark, New Jersey   6/1999
 * Bookkeeping, typing, English and business math.

References
Furnished upon request

Eyes on the Prize

Liroy Rise Jr.
316-317 Osborne Terrace * Newark, New Jersey 07232
(201) 646-3349

Objective: Position as Secretary/Clerical/Administrative Assistant.

Highlights of Qualifications
* 4 years experience as Administrative Assistant.
* 3 years secretarial experience and typed 55 words per minute.

Technical Skills:
* Microsoft Office 2003/2007, Lotus 123, and Windows 98/2000/XP.

Clerical Word Processing Training:
* Interpersonal/Communication Skills, Telephone Techniques, Time Management & Word Processing.
* **Records management**: alphabetic, numeric, subject and geographical filing.
* **Financial applications**: Recording petty cash, deposit slips, reconciling bank statements, accounts receivable and payable.
* Customer Service Training

Relevant Skills and Experience

Secretary/Administrative Skills:
* Prepared purchase orders, and conducted necessary follow-ups in a timely manner.
* Developed effective ways to improve the efficiency of the office.
* Handled payroll on a weekly basis for 90 employees.
* Assisted customers and employees with job related problems.

Record Clerk:
* Updated, handled military records and assisted service members.

Inventory Controller:
* Maintained supplies that were distributed to various business complexes.
* Developed a system to maintain accuracy of supplies.

Employment History

1994-present	**Secretary**	Executive Temp., Gateway, Newark, New Jersey
1989-1993	**Inventory Controller**	Tri-Maintenance, Maplewood, New Jersey
1984-1989	**Secretary**	Upsala College, East Orange, New Jersey
1981-1986	**Administrative Asst.**	U.S. Army, Fort-Ord, California

Education
Certificate, Clerical Word Processing-CareerWorks, Inc., Newark, New Jersey   1/1995
Diploma, Business/College Prep-Clifford J. Scott, Newark, New Jersey   1982
Communication-Tempo University-New York, New York   1981

Montego F. R. Craddock

Kilawantaa Noubee
299 Clifton Avenue
Newark, New Jersey

Telephone:
(202) 342-5678

HIGHLIGHTS OF QUALIFICATIONS
♦ Over 20 years experience as a Teacher and Lecturer.
♦ 3 years experience in supervision and administration.
  ♦ Certification in Education Administration.
  ♦ Proficient interpersonal/communication.

TECHNICAL SKILLS
MOS Certified (Microsoft Office 2003/2007), Lotus 123, Windows 98/2000/XP/Vista, Desktop Publishing, Peach Tree, Type 45 wpm with accuracy, medical technology, proof reading, transcription, faxing/coping, word processing and data processing.

PROFESSIONAL EXPERIENCE

LECTURER/ADMINISTRATOR: (Teacher's College)
Lectures on the principals and practice of education, approaches to teaching various disciplines, psychology, applied to teaching, measurement, evaluation techniques and diagnostic skills.

♦ Clinical supervision of teachers during practice in the field.
♦ Conducted team building exercise with guidance, and curriculum groups for the purpose of achieving institutional goals.
♦ Guidance Counselor to groups of students each year.
♦ Contributed to the formulation of college policies and their implementation.
♦ Coordinated cultural, religious and sporting activities within groups.
♦ Designed and developed curriculums for Arts, Handcrafts and Education.
♦ External examiner for Practice Teaching for the Board of Teacher Training.

JUNIOR SECONDARY SCHOOL:
♦ Taught Arts/Crafts to students from Grade 6 to 9.
♦ Coordinated Co-curricular activities. Guided and counseled students.

ELEMENTARY SCHOOL:
♦ Taught all disciplines to pupils ages 4 to 11. Coordinated religious and sporting activities.

SUPERVISION:
♦ Supervised a staff of waitresses, and bus persons at the Hilton Gateway Towers in Newark, New Jersey.
♦ Addressed complaints and concerns of the guests.
♦ Supervised students and teachers at the Teacher's College.

Eyes on the Prize

EMPLOYMENT HISTORY

1993-1994	**Host/Supervisor -** Hilton Gateway Towers, Newark, New Jersey
1993-1993	**Substitute Teacher -** ABC Children's Center, W. Palms Beach, Florida
1992-1993	**Teacher/Director -** Montessori Childs Center, Palms Beach Gardens, Florida
1991-1992	**Customer SVC /Admin., Asst. -** Ramsahags Hardware, Pipuro, Trinidad
1987-1992	**Lecturer-** Valsiyn Teacher's College, Trinidad, East India
1974-1987	**Lecturer -**Coranth Teacher's College, Trinidad, East India
1972-1974	**Teacher-** Siparia Junior Secondary School, Trinidad, East India
1961-1968	**Teacher Asst. -** Dabe Handu Elementary School, Trinidad, East India

EDUCATION & PROFESSIONAL DEVELOPMENT

M.A., Education - Fillow of the College of Preceptors, London, UK   1984
B.A., Education - Fillow of the College of Preceptors, London, UK   1980
A.A., Education - Nuparima Teacher's College, Trinidad, East Indies   1977

Certificate, Clerical Word Processing- CareerWorks, Inc., Newark, NJ   1/1995
Office System Technology (4 credits) -Essex County College, Newark, NJ   12/1994
Ten Hour Child Care Training Course -Department of Health & Rehabilitative Service, Palm Beach, Florida   1993
Florida Board of Education - Statement of Eligibility for Teaching Pre K to Grade 3.
Customer Service Training- Hilton Gateway & Tower, Newark, New Jersey.

PROFESSIONAL MEMBERSHIP
- Trinidad and Tobago Unified Teacher's Association.
- Trinidad and Tobago Rehabilitation Society.
- Trinidad and Tobago Art/Craft Teacher's Association.

Electronic Resume
(E-Resume)

Job search techniques have changed and evolved over the past few years. Today, many large and medium-sized organizations are using computerized tracking systems for storing and searching applicants' resumes by keywords. Even smaller companies, those with fewer than 500 employees, are joining the competition. This means job applicants must apply the rules for e-resumes; if not, opportunities might be missed.

What happens when a resume is scanned?

"To scan your resume an employer will use a scanner which looks like a compact copy machine.

Your resume is placed on the sheet of glass inside the scanner and an OCR (optical character reading) program is used to read the text of your resume, which is then stored in a database. When an employer is ready to hire, he or she can specify the type of experience, skills or education needed for a particular position. This information is then used to sort all resumes in the employer's databank. Any resumes that match the criteria are selected and printed. Key **job titles, skills**, areas of **experience** and **education** are some components that can be **extremely important** in having your resume sorted and pulled from thousands of scanned resumes. Therefore, you need to design your resume to be scanned correctly by both older and newer scanning software.

Montego F. R. Craddock

The following are tips for creating a resume that can be accurately scanned and stored in all systems:

- Always print your resume on white or very light-colored paper. Never use colored or patterned paper for your resume.
- Use 8 1/2 by 11 inch paper. Never use formats that are printed in a folder style or on 11 X 17 paper.
- Send your resume flat in a large envelope. Do not fold or staple it.
- Use a standard sans serif typeface such as Helvetica or Arial.
- Use a font that is 10 to 14 points in size.
- Your name should be the very first line on your resume. Do not have any other information on this line.
- Each phone number should be placed on a separate line and your address should be typed in standard format.
- Don't ever condense spacing between letters to try to save space. Each letter should be separate and not touch another.
- It is okay to use boldface and capitals to highlight certain sections of your resume, however; make sure the letters do not touch.
- Never use underlines.
- Don't use vertical lines, boxes, or graphics. Horizontal lines are generally okay, but make certain that they do not touch the text.
- Most OCR software can handle bullets but use them sparingly.
- Always send crisp originals of your resume. Photocopies do not scan well. You should never fax your resume, but if you have no other choice, use fine resolution mode.
- If the employer gives specific instructions for formatting your resume, FOLLOW THEM!

"ASCII texts resume - Always have an up-to-date text version of your resume on disk or flash drive. This is the fastest way to contact potential employers and to apply for jobs advertised online. You must also have a text version of your resume if you wish to post in online resume databanks. Because the text versions of your resume will almost always end up in a searchable database, you should ALWAYS use a keyword format."
Source: Distinctive Documents Web site at
www.distinctiveweb.com/elecresume.htm

Eyes on the Prize

Exercise: Complete the following worksheets to start a rough draft of your resume. Remember you will be using some of the information you compiled on **pages 1, 2, 3, 5, 6, 7 and 8.** If you decide to use the chronological format, make sure to include all necessary dates. The functional format excludes dates, and the combination format uses dates where there is consistency and avoids date where there are gaps. Avoid gaps on your resume by not writing specific dates. Instead, write the total number of months or years. **Example:** (6 months, 1 year, 4 years, etc.)

RESUME WORK SHEET

Your Name_____

Address_____

City, State, Zip Code_____

Telephone Number (   )_____

OBJECTIVE:_____

_____

(Circle One)

OFFICE SKILLS, OR HIGHLIGHTS OF QUALIFICATION, OR SUMMARY OF QUALIFICATIONS

*_____

Montego F. R. Craddock

* _____

* _____

(Circle One)

EMPLOYMENT HISTORY, PROFESSIONAL
EXPERIENCE, WORK EXPERIENCE

Dates: To_____ From_____

Name of Company, City and State_____

Job Title:_____

Accomplishments:

* _____

* _____

* _____

Responsibilities:

* _____

* _____

* _____

* _____

Eyes on the Prize

Dates To_____ **From**_____

Name of Company, City, and State_____

Job Title:_____

Accomplishments:

* _____

* _____

* _____

Responsibilities:

* _____

* _____

* _____

* _____

Dates: To_____ **From**_____

Name of the Company, City, and State:_____

Job Title:_____

Accomplishments:
* _____

* _____

Montego F. R. Craddock

* _____

Responsibilities:

* _____

* _____

* _____

* _____

Dates: To_____   From_____

Name of the Company, City, and State_____

Job Title_____

Accomplishments:
* _____

* _____

* _____

Responsibilities:
* _____

* _____

* _____

* _____

Eyes on the Prize

EDUCATION

(Write Schools in Chronological Order)

Degree or Certification in what?_____,

Name of School,

City, State, and Date graduated or will graduate:_____

Courses:_____

Accomplishments:_____

Degree or Certification in what?_____,

Name of School,

City, State, and Date graduated or will graduate:_____

Courses:_____

Accomplishments:_____

Degree or Certification in what?_____,

Name of School,

City, State, and Date graduated or will graduate:_____

Courses:_____

Accomplishments:_____

Montego F. R. Craddock

Degree or Certification in what?_____,

Name of School

City, State, and Date graduated or will graduate:_____

Courses:_____

Accomplishments:_____

Note: List courses, or training that relate to the position you want.

MEMBERSHIPS
(Related to field)

Name, City, State_____

Name, City, State_____

Name, City, State_____

REFERENCES AVAILABLE UPON REQUEST
(Not mandatory to have in your resume, unless you have adequate space)

Some of the sample resumes may look different from the traditional styles of resumes you are familiar with. In a labor market where there is tremendous competition due to high unemployment and changing technology, one must be creative to avoid getting lost in a pile of resumes. Remember, cover letters and resumes are marketing tools; they should be developed with that thought in mind.

Eyes on the Prize

Companies receive hundreds of resumes. You want your resume to outshine the others. So, you cannot write an **ordinary** resume, but you must write an **extra-ordinary** one to get attention. If they all look the same there is no need for you to send yours.

Choose to be **different.** If you want to **soar** like an **eagle** you can't hang around with pigeons. There is no specific order in which an interviewer will review a stack of resumes. If your resume looks different, it will **capture** his **attention** and might be read first.

Interviewing Techniques

The **ninth step** in preparing to win the job is to be able to effectively sell yourself to the interviewer, by persuading him or her that you are the best person for the position.

How is this done? **Claiming the job and preparation!**

You will gather information from the previous chapters in this workbook to write your **Plan of Action**.

THE PLAN

After researching your field of interest, analyze your strengths and improve any weaknesses that can detract from your presentation and/or job performance. You are now ready to begin job searching. See the next few pages for a sample plan of action.

Use Job Resources on pages 9 to 12. This must be done **each day** for maximum results. There is no time for stopping halfway. You must do what's required and then some if you want to win the job. It may cost money, but if the result is a job, it is well worth the effort. Most libraries have the latest publications and newspapers that you can read at no cost to you except your time.

Use various resources: networking, newspaper, cold calling, pounding the pavement, and employment agencies. With effort, you are sure to get interviews. **Before the interview, make sure you research the company and/or the industry in which it's competing**.

Use the sample log sheets on the next two pages to assist you in keeping track of your contacts. You can make copies of the original log sheet. Keeping records is important. When you are mailing cover letters and resumes, make copies or make a notation on your log of the paperwork you sent, to keep for your records.

DATE	NAME & ADDRESS	TELEPHONE #	COMMENTS

COMPANY NAME & ADDRESS	DATE	CONTACT PERSON	TELEPHONE NUMBER	INTERVIEW DATE	COMPLETE APPLICATION	MAIL/FAX/E-MAIL COVER LETTER AND RESUME

Eyes on the Prize

It's not the woman or man it's the plan, it's not the rap but the map.

When using cold calling techniques to gain job opportunities, develop some type of script to practice before you make your contacts. Good phone etiquette is essential to being successful at convincing the personnel manager (or whoever is in charge of hiring for the position) that you are an excellent candidate. **Remember, be persistent, courteous, and don't be quick to give up.** Below is a sample phone script.

PHONE SCRIPT

Good morning, (afternoon, or evening), my name is_____
_____ **. Who is the**

person in charge of hiring for_____
? (Name of the position)

Can you spell his or her name please? _____
May I speak with Mr. or

Ms._____(Name   of   the   Person)?
Please!

If asked the reason for the call, inform the receptionist or secretary and be courteous because he can be very helpful. If the person is unavailable, ask about the best times to call. If the company is not hiring, ask when they might be hiring. If that is soon, call back to set up an interview. If not, ask if you can mail, e-mail, or fax your resume to the person in charge of hiring for that position. If you are able to speak with the person doing the hiring, be prepared to persuade that person over the phone to give you an interview.

Introduce yourself the same way you spoke to the receptionist or secretary. **Example:** Good Morning Mr. or Ms. Doe, my name is Mary Jane and I am interested in seeking a manager position with your company. I am a recent graduate with a degree in Management Science. I have several years' experience as a manager supervising, planning, budgeting, and controlling. My research tells me that this company is known for its Quality Control Management. I feel my skills meet those requirements. If you have any openings I would like to set up an interview at your convenience to discuss in detail how I can be an asset to your organization. Wait for his response. If the company is not hiring, ask if you might send your cover letter and resume for future consideration. Ask the interviewer if he knows of other companies that might be hiring.

If you are able to arrange an interview, make sure you allow sufficient time to do research on the company or its industry. **Example:** If you spoke with the interviewer on Monday and he wants to arrange an interview the same day, ask if you can arrange it for Tuesday or Wednesday instead. If not, arrange it later that day so you have some time to prepare yourself. When you have several interviews in one day, allow adequate time between appointments. Before the interview, familiarize yourself with your resume.

THE INTERVIEW

Make sure to arrive **30 minutes** early. Allow adequate time for flat tires and traffic congestion. Or, if you are taking public transportation, call to get their schedule to assure your punctual arrival. The fastest way to lose credibility is to be late for an interview. There is no legitimate excuse other than your death.

Why be present **30 minutes** before an interview, rather than the **15 minutes** most consultants recommend? I want you to arrive **30 minutes** before the interview, but don't walk into the office just then, because you will be putting pressure on the interviewer to see you before your scheduled appointment. Take the **first five minutes** to get yourself together. Go to the restroom to make sure you look perfect. For the **next five minutes,** try to relax by taking deep breaths. Use the **last five minutes** to arrive **15 minutes** before the appointment, to make a good impression.

THE INTERVIEW SCENE

Go to the interview with this attitude: "It's not what the company can do for me, but what I can do for the company." You already know what the company can do for you through your research.

Make sure you have the following items with you at the interview:

1. Driver's License
2. Social Security card
3. Three pens with black ink
4. A legal pad, or palm pilot
5. Daily Reminder (appointment book, or palm pilot) This shows the interviewer that you are organized.
6. Copies of your resume, reference sheet, or letters of recommendation.
7. Business card (If you don't have one, create one.)

Montego F. R. Craddock

THE INTERVIEW SCENE

1. The screening process begins the moment you walk through the door. The first thing the interviewer will notice is your appearance. Be at your best, look conservative, and remember navy blue or gray the preferred colors.

2. When you walk through the door 15 minutes before the scheduled interview, **smile** and **introduce** yourself to the secretary or receptionist. **Example:** Good morning! (afternoon!, evening!) My name is_____ _____, and I have an interview with Ms. (Mr.) **John Brown** at 9:00 a.m. (This is important because the secretary or receptionist can make you or break you. The interviewer might ask him or for his opinion of you.) At this time you might be requested to complete a job application. It should take approximately 15 minutes if you are prepared with your information index card as discussed on **page 34,** and resume.

3. Remember, claim the job: you have one goal in mind, to persuade the interviewer you are the best candidate for the position. After completing the application, several things can take place. Either you are escorted to the interviewer's office or he will come and get you. **Be prepared to smile, introduce yourself, give a firm hand shake, and show eye contact to reveal confidence. Example:** Good morning (afternoon, evening) my name is_____.

4. Don't be seated until you are **asked**. Sit upright in the chair. Don't lounge in the chair, or have your legs wide open. Keep your legs together. If you are female, you can cross your legs.

5. If you smoke, don't, even if you're told it's OK.

6. Don't chew gum or eat candy during the interview.

7. Make sure to have extra copies of your resume just in case the interviewer doesn't have it present.

8. Take out your legal pad to write notes of important issues you may want to use in your thank you letter or acceptance letter or letter of refusal.

9. If the interviewer is impressed he will want references to verify your work ethic. Be sure to get the consent of your references before you use them. A letter of recommendation adds more credibility then just a list of names. In a letter of recommendation the author will write briefly about your work ethic and character. This kind of letter is ideal to have if the company you worked for has gone out of business. If you can't get a letter of recommendation, then create a reference sheet. **See sample on next page:**

REFERENCES

Mr. John Mitchell, Manager
Storm's International
23 West Ruin Road
North, New Jersey 09876
(209) 675-9878

Ms. Mary Brown, Personnel Manager
S & B Associates
11 South Munn Road
Littleton, New Jersey 09876
(609) 769-4321

Ms. Ebby Walkins, Counselor
Rutgers University
33 Washington St.
Newark, New Jersey
(201) 824-4567

---

10. Usually the interviewer is aware that you are nervous, so to break the ice, he may want to engage in small talk. **Note:** Make sure you are familiar with current events since they might be the subject of the small talk.

11. You cannot anticipate every question that might be asked because each interviewer is different. You might get an interviewer who is relaxed, conservative, democratic, or autocratic. Again, be prepared. Someone said, "It's better to be prepared for an opportunity and not have one, then have an opportunity and not be prepared." Even if the interviewer is very sociable don't forget you are at an interview.

Eyes on the Prize

There are common questions that most interviewers ask. Listed below are samples you might expect. Questions can fall into the following categories: **Education, Work Experience, Career Goals, and Personality.** Be prepared to discuss these topics.

EDUCATION

1. Why did you attend_____? (college or trade school)
2. What was your grade point average?
3. What subjects did you enjoy the most? The least? Why?
4. What leadership position do you hold or you have held?
5. Why was your grade so low or high?
6. Did you do the best you could in school? If not why not?

> Success is more likely when you strive to deserve it than when you strive to attain it
>
> -Anonymous

WORK EXPERIENCE

1. What were your major achievements in each of your past jobs?
2. Why did you change jobs before?
3. Why do you want to leave your current job?
4. Do you prefer working with others or alone?
5. How do others view your work?
6. How do you deal with stressful situations?
7. How well do you work under deadline?
8. Are you a team player?

9. What will you bring to this position that another candidate won't?
10. How long have you been looking for another job?
11. How soon can you begin work?
12. What were your responsibilities?
13. What functions do you enjoy the most?
14. What is a typical work day like?
15. How will you use your previous work experience to help improve our company?
16. What did you like about your boss? Dislike?
17. Have you ever been fired? Why?

The pursuit of excellence is gratifying and healthy; the pursuit of perfection is frustrating, neurotic, and a terrible waste of time.
-Anonymous

CAREER GOALS

1. Why do you want to join our organization? (To effectively answer this, you must have done research.)
2. Why do you think you are qualified for this position?
3. Why are you looking for another job?
4. Where do you see yourself three years from now within our organization?
5. Why should we hire you?
6. What ideally would you like to do?
7. What is the lowest pay you will accept?
8. What do you want to be doing five years from now?
9. How much do you think you are worth for this job?
10. Why do you want to make a career change?

11. How much do you want to be making five years from now?
12. What attracted you to our company?
13. How do you feel about relocating, traveling, working over-time, and spending weekends in the office?
14. What are your short-range and long-range goals?
15. What other types of jobs are you considering? Other than companies?
16. How long do you expect to stay with our company?

PERSONALITY

1. Tell me something about yourself.
2. What are your major weaknesses? Your major strengths?
3. What do you do in your spare time? Any hobbies?
4. What causes you to lose your temper?
5. What types of books do you read?
6. Tell me about your management philosophy?
7. What types of people do you prefer working with?
8. Do you consider yourself to be someone who takes greater initiative than others?
9. Are you a self-starter?
10. What type of person would you hire?

OTHER CONSIDERATIONS

1. Who are your references?
2. If you could change your life what would you do dif-ferently?
3. How_____ (creative, analytical, tactful, etc.) are you?
4. What role does your family play in your career?

ILLEGAL QUESTIONS

Although we have laws to protect us (Title VII of the Civil Rights Act of 1964 makes discrimination illegal on the basis of sex, religion, or national origin), there are some people who will ask inappropriate questions anyway, out of ignorance. Some may ask just to see how you respond under pressure.

If you are asked discriminatory questions and decide to answer them, be tactful and professional. Or say thanks, but no thanks, and leave the interview. File a complaint. Again, you must decide whether to answer the question or refuse to disclose this information.

Here is a list of illegal questions:
1. Are you married? Single? Separated? Divorced?
2. Do you have any children? How many?
3. Do you go to church regularly?
4. Do you own or rent your home?
5. Do you have many debts?
6. What social or political group you belong to?
7. What does your spouse think about your career?
8. Are you living with anyone?
9. Are you practicing birth control?
10. How old are you?
11. Were you ever arrested?
12. How much do you weigh?
13. How much insurance do you have?
14. How tall are you?

Unless these questions have legitimate bearing, and the company can prove they do in court, it is illegal for them to be asked during a pre-employment interview.

Eyes on the Prize

FINAL COMMENTS

When answering questions about your accomplishments, use **examples, illustrations, testimonials, descriptions, statistics, definitions, and comparisons**. It helps to prove your assertions. You also gain an advantage in oral presentation over applicants who don't.

Remember, always use **eye contact**! Nod your head from time to time and **smile occasionally**, and no **fake smiles**, please! It is important to use the language of your chosen career field when answering questions. At some point the interviewer will ask if you have any questions. The worst comment you can make is "no" (it shows lack of interest). **The best questions are the ones from your research**. They are the most impressive. After you've researched the company, take time to write well thought-out questions.
The following are some basic questions you can ask on an interview:

1. Why is the position open?
2. Is it a new position?
3. If not why did the person who held it previously leave?
4. How important is this position to the organization?
5. How would you evaluate the financial soundness and growth potential of this company?
6. If you had to briefly describe this organization, what would you say? What about its employees? Its managers and supervisors? Its performance evaluation systems? Its promotion practices?
7. What would be my most important duties? Responsibilities?
8. What type of projects would I be working with?
9. What will be the major challenges for the person who is hired?

10. To what extent does the company promote from within versus hiring from the outside?
11. What plans for expansion (or cutbacks) are in the immediate future? What effect will these plans have on the position or the department in which it is located?
12. On the average, how long do most employees stay with this company?

Toward the end of the interview, ask when a decision will be made, and if you may call if you are not contacted. After this first meeting, there might be a second interview with the person responsible to make the final decision. Sometimes you may be required to have several interviews before a decision is made. Don't worry about the number of people who interview you, it's the quality you present to them that will determine success. If there is a second interview, take out your daily reminder appointment book to write down any necessary information about the person who will interview you. The appointment book or palm pilot shows you are organized. Make sure you take time to reveal it. Before leaving be sure to **thank** the interviewer and give a firm handshake.

Note: People who don't have extensive work experience should consider using a portfolio to show their best work (from school, projects, essays, typed correspondence, etc.) My Clerical Word Processing Class used this technique and was very successful.

Example: Your portfolio will contain the following:

1st page: Your resume.
2nd page: Letters of recommendation, or reference sheet showed on page 91 and 92.
3rd page: Special awards.
4th page: Samples of your best work performed in class training: assignments, projects, spreadsheets, graphics, charts, tables, etc.
A person with extensive experience and education may not need a portfolio; it depends on the nature of the job.

"Be thankful for prob-
lems. If they were less
difficult, someone with
less ability might have
your job."

-Bits & Pieces

Thank You Letter

The **tenth step** in preparing to win the job is to send a thank-you letter immediately after the interview. Write down pertinent information you learned during the interview. You will use this information in your thank-you letter and to compare job offers. Send your thank-you letter the same day of the interview, or the following morning, for the following reasons:

1. To show courtesy, for giving you the opportunity to be interviewed, and to remind the interviewer why you are the better candidate.

2. To keep your name on the interviewer's mind.

3. To give you a competitive edge. Most applicants don't take the time to send a thank you letter.

4. To possibly change the interviewer's perception of you. It's possible that you were on the interviewer's "maybe" list or were not considered for the job, but because you have taken the time to send a thank-you letter he might change his mind. This is a maybe!

See a sample **thank- you letter on the next page**.

How often we forget the little words of thanks, praise, or encouragement. When we look back at our life we remember not the gifts we been given, but the smile, the kiss, the praise that has helped and enriched us. We must pray not to forget to give freely these "little things" to everyone we meet today.

——Barbra Cartland

Bob Miller
2789 Style Road
Charlotte, NC 28101
(234) 567-7896

August 7, 2008

Mr. Vicint Vallone
Personnel Manager
Veltex Industries Inc.
75 Commercial Drive
Leigh, NC 28210

Dear Mr. Vallone:

Thank you again for the opportunity to interview for the bookkeeping position on September 24, 2007. I appreciated your hospitality and enjoyed meeting with you and members of your staff.

The interview convinced me of how compatible my background, interest, and skills are with the goals of Veltex Industries. I am confident that my qualifications would enable me to perform the duties to everyone's advantage.

I look forward to hearing from you soon.

Sincerely,

Bob Miller

Salary Negotiation

One of the ways a company may screen applicants is to ask about salary preference before the interview. Be careful of this question. If it is asked on the application, it might mean the company is on a budget and you will be screened out if you quote a salary that's too high. On the other hand, if you quote too low, you may end up being underpaid.

This is why research is important—to give you an idea of what is a competitive salary, so you can use it as a basis to negotiate.

Avoid this question if you don't have an interview or receive a job offer. Why? You have no leverage to negotiate if you haven't received a job offer. If you were making job inquires by phone and the first question you were asked concerned salary, this is what you might say to avoid answering the question:

Possible answer: "At this time I'd rather not discuss salary, unless you're sure I am the right person for the position. I'm sure whatever you are paying is competitive." If you must, say that your salary needs are negotiable, or ask what they are currently paying for the position. What you want is an interview to prove your worth.

The salary question is awkward for many applicants who are reluctant to talk about money. They think one must take what is offered because salaries are set by employers. Such thinking is unfortunate, because it means many people are paid less than they're worth. Except for many entry-level positions for people without experience, salary is seldom predetermined. Most employers have some flexibility to negotiate salary. While they do not try to exploit applicants, neither do they want to pay applicants more than the work warrants. Salaries are usually assigned to positions or jobs rather than to individuals. You should attempt to establish your value in the eyes of the employer rather than accept a salary figure for the job.

Develop a personal budget to help you determine what salary is acceptable.

You should never ask about salary prior to being offered the job, even though it is one of your major concerns. Try to let the employer initiate the salary question. When he or she does, take your time. Don't appear too anxious. While you know based on your previous research approximately what the employer will offer, try to get the employer to state a figure first. If you do this you will be in a stronger negotiating position. When the salary questions arises, assuming you cannot or do not want to put it off until later, your first step should be to clearly summarize the job responsibilities/duties as you understand them. You are attempting to do two things:

1. Seek clarification from the interviewer as to the actual job and all it involves.

2. Stress the level of skills required in the most positive way. In other words, you emphasize the value and worth of this position to the organization.

After you have proved you can be an asset to the organization, the last phase of the interview process is to receive a job offer. What are you worth? What salary are you willing to accept? How are you going to get more than the employer is willing to offer? These are the questions you should ask yourself. You should prepare a plan of action to answer the questions.

What are your salary requirements?

Eyes on the Prize

Your first response should be to outline the responsibilities of the position:

Let me see if I comprehend all that is involved with this position. I would be expected to_____.

Have I discussed everything or are there some other responsibilities I should know about?

This reply focuses the salary question around the worth of the position. After the interviewer responds to your final question, answer the initial salary question in this manner:

What is the standard range in your company for a position such as this?

This question establishes the worth as well as the range for the position or job. The employer usually will tell you the requested salary range. Once he or she does, depending on how you feel about the figure, you can follow up with another question.

What would be the standard salary range for someone with my qualifications?

This question further attempts to establish the worth of the individual rather than that of the position. This line of questioning will yield the salary expectations of the employer without revealing your desired salary figure or range.

Example: If the employer indicates he or she is prepared to offer $38,000 to $44,000 and these figures are consistent with the salary data you gathered, you should establish common ground for negotiation, by placing your salary range into the employer's range.

Yes, that does come within the proximity of what I was expecting. I was thinking $41,000 to $47,000.

Note: If interviewer declines your salary requirement and you still want to work for them, request reevaluation after ninety days to demonstrate your worth to the company, or try to negotiate some benefits that are not standard. Remember, after you've been of-fered a position is the time when you have the greatest leverage to negotiate salary. Be realistic.

Letter of Acceptance

If you are made a job offer and you accept, write a letter of acceptance to confirm what was discussed and negotiated. Sometimes the company will send you a letter of acceptance. The procedure for such a letter is to begin by accepting the job you have been offered. Identify the job title, state the exact salary and benefit package, so there will be no confusion on these important points.

The second paragraph might discuss moving or reporting dates. These details will vary depending on the nature of the job offer. See sample on the next page.

Bob Miller
2789 Style Road
Charlotte, NC 28210
(223) 345-6798

April 29, 2007

Ms. Mary Sue
Personnel Manager
Associates Corporation
78 Commerce Street
Longville, NC 78750

Dear Ms. Sue:

I am pleased to accept your offer of $19,500, with benefits, as a word processor at Associates Corporation.

After graduation I will be ready to report to work on May 1, 2007.

I look forward to what I am sure will be a rewarding future.

Sincerely,

Bob Miller

Job Rejection
Follow-up Letter

Write a job rejection follow-up letter if you have been declined a position, and want to be considered for future employment. See sample on the next page.

Montego F. R. Craddock

Bob Miller
12 River Road
Valley, NJ 07088
(609) 456-6789

August 7, 2008

Mr. Paul Moorse, President
L & L Associates
21 Southern Road
St. Louis, MO 53178

Dear Mr. Moorse:

I appreciated your consideration for the marketing position.

While I am disappointed at not being selected, I learned a great deal about your organization and enjoyed meeting with you and your staff.

Please keep me in mind for future consideration. I have a strong interest in your organization. I believe we would work well together. I will be closely following the progress of your organization over the coming months.

Perhaps we will be in touch with each other at some later date.

Sincerely,

Bob Miller

Job Refusal Letter

If you receive more than one job offer, and you have made a decision on which company you want to work for, send the other companies a letter of refusal. Sometimes when the company values your skills they might make a counter offer to persuade you to work for them.

See sample Letter of Refusal on the next page.

Montego F. R. Craddock

Bob Miller
2647 Peter Roads
Glen Oak, NJ 07338
(609) 741-3421

August 7, 2008

Mr. John Lance
Personnel Manager
Community Inc.
32 Park Drive
Westville, MA 02174

Dear Mr. Lance:

I enjoyed talking with you about your opening for Data Entry Operator and I was delighted to receive your offer. Although I have given the offer serious thought, I have decided to accept a position with another communications company.

The job I have chosen will provide me with a greater variety of duties, which I feel will develop my skills more fully in the long run. The company has offered me a better monetary package.

I appreciated your consideration and I am sure I would have enjoyed working for your company.

Sincerely,

Bob Miller

Summary

EYES ON THE PRIZE means that, through your trials and tribulations in search for 21st century jobs, never lose sight of the position you want. Prepare and develop a plan of action. Claim it and you will win it! To boldly go where no woman or man has gone before—I am not talking about "Star-Trek" or "The Next Generation," but the idea is similar.

Winning the job is preparing oneself to succeed in the labor force, by having a positive attitude, assertiveness, persistence, patience, using your strengths, improving your weakness, researching the job/company, using job search resources, wearing the appropriate dress attire, completing the job application neatly/accurately, writing effective cover letter/resume, knowing how to sell yourself, sending a thank you letter, and negotiating your salary. All of these steps equal guaranteed success.

www.ingramcontent.com/pod-product-compliance
Lightning Source LLC
Chambersburg PA
CBHW022007170526
45157CB00003B/1188